FLOOD

Heinemann
LIBRARY

Catherine Chambers

www.heinemann.co.uk/library
Visit our website to find out more information about **Heinemann Library** books.

To order:

 Phone ++44 (0)1865 888066

 Send a fax to ++44 (0)1865 314091

 Visit the Heinemann Bookshop at www.heinemann.co.uk/library to browse our catalogue and order online.

First published in Great Britain by Heinemann Library, Halley Court, Jordan Hill, Oxford OX2 8EJ, a division of Reed Educational and Professional Publishing Ltd. Heinemann is a registered trademark of Reed Educational & Professional Publishing Ltd.

OXFORD MELBOURNE AUCKLAND JOHANNESBURG BLANTYRE GABORONE IBADAN PORTSMOUTH NH (USA) CHICAGO

Designed by Visual Image
Illustration by Paul Bale
Originated by Ambassador Litho Ltd.
Printed and bound in South China.

ISBN 0 431 15065 6

06 05 04 03 02
10 9 8 7 6 5 4 3 2 1

British Library Cataloguing in Publication Data

Chambers, Catherine
Flood. – (Wild Weather)
1. Floods – Juvenile literature
I. Title
551.4'89
ISBN 0431150656

Acknowledgements

The Publishers would like to thank the following for permission to reproduce photographs: Ardea p5, Corbis pp14, 16, 17, 23, 24, 28, Ecoscene pp4, 8, 10, 12, 25, 29, EPA (PA photos) p22, Oxford Scientific Films pp9, 11, 19, PA Photos pp21, 27, Reuters pp13, 18, Rex Features p26, Robert Harding Picture Library pp15, 20, Still Pictures p7.

The Publishers would like to thank the Met Office for their assistance with the preparation of this book.

Cover photograph reproduced with permission of Robert Harding Picture Library.

Every effort has been made to contact copyright holders of any material reproduced in this book. Any omissions will be rectified in subsequent printings if notice is given to the Publisher.

Any words appearing in the text in bold, **like this**, are explained in the Glossary.

Contents

What is a flood? 4

Where do floods happen? 6

Heavy rain 8

Why do floods happen? 10

What are floods like? 12

Mississippi River floods 14

Harmful floods 16

Helpful floods 18

Preparing for floods 20

Coping with floods 22

Living with floods 24

To the rescue! 26

Adapting to floods 28

Fact file 30

Glossary 31

Index 32

What is a flood?

A flood is when water covers the land. Heavy rain makes river waters spill over their **banks**. Storms can make huge sea waves that flood the coast.

This is North Dakota in the United States. The waters of the great Red River have burst over the banks and flooded fields and buildings. People have been forced to leave their homes.

5

Where do floods happen?

Floods happen mostly where there are lots of storms. Storms bring heavy rain and strong winds. This can cause rivers to flood.

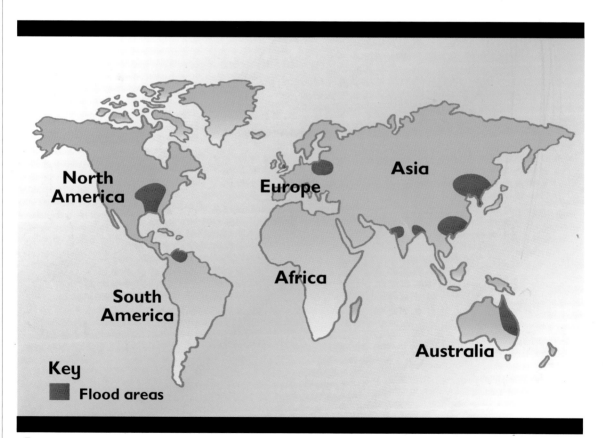

North America

Europe

Asia

South America

Africa

Australia

Key

Flood areas

This flood is in the country of Bangladesh.
Bangladesh gets a lot of heavy rain from June to
September. This time is called the wet monsoon
season. Floods often happen in Bangladesh.

Heavy rain

Winds blow over the sea. They pick up tiny drops of **water vapour**. Cold air high above cools the water vapour. It forms heavy drops of water. These drops fall as rain.

Clouds are made up of water vapour that has
been cooled. Large, dark clouds hold a lot of
water vapour. These clouds can bring heavy
rain and sudden floods.

Why do floods happen?

This is a river **flood plain**. When heavy rain falls the river can become too full. The water rises above the **banks** and spills on to the flood plain.

Strong winds blow across the sea during storms.
This makes the water into huge waves. These
rise over the shore and cause floods along
the coast.

What are floods like?

Sometimes floodwaters rise slowly. People have time to get ready for the flood. At other times floodwaters rise quickly. People and cars get caught in the flood.

The water makes anything inside buildings get
wet. Some things are washed away. The water
also brings a lot of dirt. This dirt has been
picked up by the floodwaters.

Mississippi River floods

This is the town of Bellevue in the United States. The town lies on the **flood plain** of the great Mississippi River. **Flood defences** have been built to try and stop the floods.

In 1993 there was a lot of rain and the river began to flood over its **banks**. The walls built to stop the floods broke. The town was flooded. All the people had to leave their homes.

Harmful floods

Floodwaters trap people and animals. Roads and bridges are flooded and broken. It can be harder to find fresh food or clean **drinking water**.

Huge waves have flooded this coast. Boats and buildings are broken. Roads are covered in sand and stones. Fish, seabirds and seaweed are washed up onto the shore.

Helpful floods

Here in Bangladesh, plants rot in the floodwaters. The rotted plants in the water help to make **fertile** soil. Rice **crops** grow well in this soil.

A river flows very fast when there is a lot of
rain. The fast river washes down a lot of mud.
The mud settles on flooded fields. This can make
the soil in these fields more fertile.

Preparing for floods

Weather stations ask radio and television stations to warn people about floods. The most serious warning is the **flood alert**. This warns people to get ready for floods.

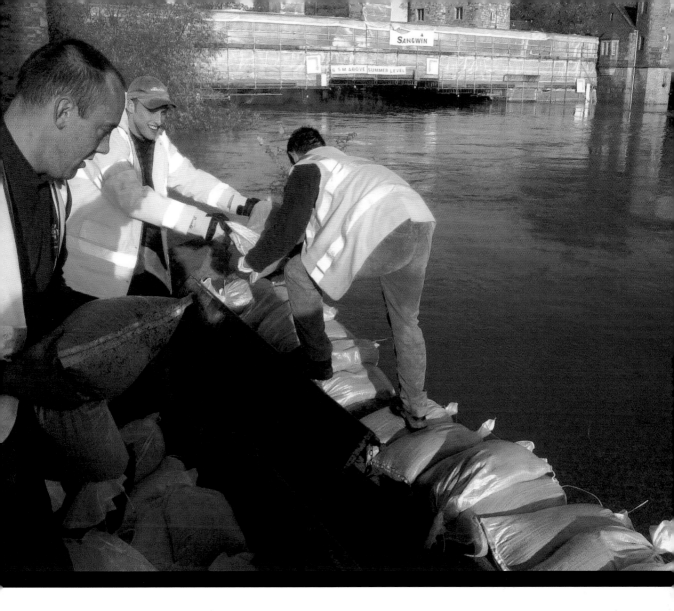

People move their furniture upstairs. They switch off the electricity. Sandbags are stacked against doors. This stops water from getting in. Some people leave their homes.

Coping with floods

In some countries there are bad floods nearly every year. So **flood shelters** are built on high ground. People hurry to these shelters when there is a flood.

Floodwaters can cover roads for many days.
The water stops car and bus engines from
working. So people can only travel around by
boat or by air.

Living with floods

This is an area that often floods. So people have built **platforms** on **stilts**. Cows, chickens and other livestock are kept safe until the floodwaters go down.

Rice is a **crop** that grows in flooded fields, but heavy flooding destroys rice and other crops. They are battered by the flowing water. Then they rot in the ground.

To the rescue!

The country of Mozambique was badly flooded in 2000. Helicopters rescued people from trees and high ground. They dropped food and equipment to make clean **drinking water**.

Sea **lifeboats** are being used to rescue these
people from their flooded homes. The rescuers
are taking the people to places that are above
the flood. There they will find food and warmth.

Adapting to floods

These houses are close to a river that often floods. The houses have been built on **stilts**. When the river floods the houses will be above the floodwaters.

This is a new **dam** in the country of the
Netherlands. The dam's high walls stop the flat
land below from being flooded. A road runs on
top of the walls.

Fact file

◆ The Huang Ho River in the country of China floods a lot. Flooding on the Huang Ho River has killed more people than any other flood. In 1931 nearly four million people drowned.

◆ The Earth's **climate** is changing all the time. At the moment it seems to be getting hotter. This is called 'global warming'. Some scientists think that global warming will bring more floods.

Glossary

banks sides of a river

climate usual weather in a part of the world

crops plants grown for eating, like rice or wheat

dam lake made by people for storing water

drinking water clean water that is safe to drink

fertile good for growing crops in

flood alert last flood warning before rising waters get dangerous

flood defences walls to stop floodwaters flowing on to the land

flood plain flat land along which a river winds

flood shelters buildings put up on high ground so that people can escape the floods

lifeboat boat built specially for rescuing people from dangerous waters

platforms flat floors raised above the ground

stilts tall poles that hold up platforms or buildings

water vapour water that has changed into a gas

weather station where scientists work out changes in the weather

Index

adapting to floods 24, 28–9

Bangladesh 7, 18

China 30

climate change 30

clouds 9

coastal floods 4, 11, 17

coping with floods 22–5

crops 18, 25

damage 13, 16, 17

dams 29

drinking water 16, 26

flood alerts 20

flood defences 14

flood plains 10, 14

flood shelters 22

flood areas 6

floodwaters 12, 13, 16, 18, 23, 28

global warming 30

helpful floods 18–19

lifeboats 27

monsoon season 7

Mozambique 26

Netherlands 29

preparing for floods 20–1

rain 4, 6, 7, 8, 9, 10, 15, 19

rescue action 26–7

river banks 4, 5, 10, 15

sea waves 4, 11, 17

stilt houses and platforms 24, 28

storms 4, 6, 11

United States 5, 14–15

water vapour 8, 9

weather stations 20